Early Childhood Educa

101 Ways to Play with a 2-year-old

NANOOK BOOKS

ISBN 978-1-62321-113-4

Nanook Books

www.nanookbooks.com

New York 2014

101 Ways to Play with a 2-year-old

Elaborated by
Dena Angevin, Anne Jackle,
Mary-Iola Langowski, Betty Lucky, Ben Torrent

Illustrated by
Kasia Kołodziej

Typesetting by
Magda Lena Rook

NANOOK BOOKS

Intro

A two-year-old child is no longer a helpless baby, but a little person who is able to walk and run independently, although often awkwardly, has a higher level of manual dexterity and displays a constantly developing capacity for both understanding and speaking. First and foremost, your two-year-old is very curious about the world and always ready to play. This enthusiasm for playing is an opportunity to teach your child new skills, develop imagination and creativity and most importantly — to foster happiness.

The games and activities presented in this book are adapted to the needs and abilities of a two-year-old. They are designed to support your child's natural development, combining both fun and learning: through play a child learns, e.g., colors and parts of the body, practices movement and speech, strengthens family ties and experiences cooperation with peers. The only things you need in order to play with a child are time and invention — it does not take much to bring your child and yourself a great deal of joy. Have fun!

A word about pronouns
He and she have been alternated throughout these activities,
but every activity is for boys or girls!

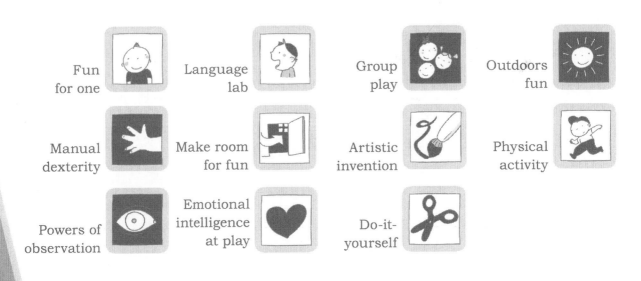

Fun for one	Language lab	Group play	Outdoors fun
Manual dexterity	Make room for fun	Artistic invention	Physical activity
Powers of observation	Emotional intelligence at play	Do-it-yourself	

Level of difficulty:　* Easy　** Moderate　*** Difficult

1

Nose to Nose

Crouch down with your child standing in front of you. When you say "Nose to nose!" get closer to one another until your noses are touching. Practice closing and opening your eyes simultaneously: seen up close, eyes may seem large as an owl's! Touch and compare other parts of your bodies in size (hands) and length (arms).

---

* This game uses touch to strengthen the ties between a parent and child.

2
Animal Book

Prepare a few sheets of colored paper, a thin ribbon, glue, scissors and color magazines. Together with your child, choose pictures of animals, cut them out and glue them on the paper sheets. Make holes and thread the sheets together with the ribbon and tie it. Your book is ready! Look through the book together, find names for the animals, and imitate the sounds they make or talk about how they look.

---

* Awakens creativity and develops the imagination.

3

Guess What

Guessing games can be played anywhere: at home, on a walk, in a doctor's waiting room or in a train. Look around and find a relatively large object of a uniform color. When you find it, say aloud and clearly: "I see a red object! Guess what it is." Your child should look around and try to guess what object you are talking about.

** Your child learns to recognize and remember colors as well as develops powers of observation.

4
Ladybug

Two-year-olds are curious about the world — they want to see and touch everything. Take your child to a park or field, and show her the small creatures that live there: butterflies, snails, ladybugs... Name and describe them. Allow your child to examine a ladybug close up by placing one on her arm. This will undoubtedly delight your child! Blow on the insect and watch as it opens its wings and flies away...which may both delight and sadden your child. Teach your child a short rhyme and encourage her to wave goodbye to the ladybug.

Ladybug, ladybug,
fly away;
Come again some
other day.

---

* A simple game that helps a child to learn respect for nature and the opportunity to commune with it.

5

Beach Bowling

Fill a few plastic bottles with water and stand them up in the sand. Remove any obstacles, and smooth the sand between you and the 'pins'. Now show your child how to roll the ball in order to knock over the bottles. Once they have been knocked down, refilling them with water will represent another attraction for your child.

---

* An exercise that improves accuracy and manual dexterity.

6
The Name Game

This is a game for a group of children who stand in a circle and hold hands. Lead the children in singing the rhyme below:

Round in a circle,
Round in a game,
Round and round,
And what's your name?

One by one the children are invited to say their names after the group says the rhyme.

---

* A simple game that encourages social interaction.

7

Cut and Paste

You will need colored and white paper as well as glue, preferably in stick form. Draw gray clouds on a piece of white paper, and ask your child to finish the drawing by pasting in pieces of paper to represent rain. If your child has difficulty tearing off small pieces of paper from an entire sheet, tear each sheet into strips, which are easier to rip.

***

** Your child practices manual dexterity and gains a sense of accomplishment from creating a picture independently.

8
Clap your Hands!

This is a good game to play with a child who has a lot of pent-up energy. Recite the rhyme found below, carrying out the actions with your child. This rhyme can incorporate other actions such as "Stomp your feet!", "Nod your head!", "Turn around!" etc.

If you're happy and you know it,
Clap your hands! (Clap, clap)
If you're happy and you know it,
Clap your hands! (Clap, clap)
If you're happy and you know it,
Then your face will surely show it, (Point to your smile)
If you're happy and you know it,
Clap your hands! (Clap, clap)

---

* Your child expends built-up energy and practices physical coordination.

9

Tales of Flying

Think up a story which features characters that can fly (e.g., a sparrow or airplane). Tell this story to your child, asking her to listen carefully. Every time something that flies appears in the story, your child should move her arms in imitation of wings.

*** A game that teaches concentration and careful listening as well as trains reflexes.

10

Breakfast

Two-year-olds like to do many things by themselves. Ask your child to make his own breakfast. Put two or three small plastic bowls on the table with tasty foods, e.g., cereal, raisins and pieces of banana. Let your child pour these ingredients into a larger bowl and mix the foods together. Add milk, stir again and breakfast is served!

---

*   Preparing a meal teaches independence and allows a child to develop confidence.

11
Hocus-Pocus!

Explain to your child that you are now a witch and your words have magical power. Slowly and clearly pronounce the incantation: "Hocus-pocus! Now stop!" Your child must stop whatever he is doing, becoming motionless and not speaking. Change roles: your child will be delighted at having the ability to immobilize you.

** Your child learns to exercise control over his body as well as emotions.

12
Pairs

Find objects that can be paired up, e.g., two teddy bears, balls, toy cars, etc. Explain the concept of a pair, and put all the objects into a bag. Now ask your child to take out each pair from the bag without looking — he should be able to find the objects using touch alone.

*** Your child learns concentration and hones the sense of touch.

13

Pop Goes the Balloon!

This is an excellent game for playing at home or outside — the more children the better. The children should stand close together in a circle and hold hands. When they hear the phrase "The balloon is growing!" the children should step away from each other as far as they can, while still holding hands, breathing in air and blowing it all out as if blowing up a balloon. When you say "Pop goes the balloon!" the children should fall down. Fun and giggling guaranteed!

---

* Develops physical coordination, exercises breathing control and deepens the bond between peers.

14

Wheelbarrow

Pretending to be a wheelbarrow is a game that is older than time. Your child gets into position on hands and knees. Hold onto your child's legs (or hips), and gently lift them up, encouraging him to walk with hands. If your child gets tired, slowly lower his legs. Don't worry if your child isn't able to 'walk' at first — with time this game will be a source of fun for both of you!

---

*   A fun exercise that teaches your child coordination.

15
Making Tracks!

Lay out a large sheet of paper on the ground, and dilute some paint on a plate with water. Ask your child to choose a car, and then the game can begin. Let your child dip the wheels of the car in the paint, place the car on the paper and...away you go! At first the car moves slowly, and then faster, makes a turn, then another, etc. What amazing tracks the wheels make! Your little artist can use a variety of cars and paint colors.

---

*   Your child learns precise hand movements and discovers the magic of combining colors.

16

Treasure Boxes

This is a game that combines fun and usefulness: you and your child will have fun while cleaning his room. You can use, for example, old shoe boxes or other containers. Segregate the smaller toys together — toy cars, stuffed animals and blocks — and place them in separate boxes. Finally, label each box with a colorful drawing or a picture cut out of a magazine of the objects inside.

---

*   Your child learns to organize his things and begins to interpret symbols — connecting the pictures with the contents of the boxes.

17

Follow the Footsteps

When you and your child are at the seaside, take a short walk on the beach. You lead, asking your child to follow in your footsteps. Walking barefoot is a real pleasure! To add more fun and difficulty, walk backwards, on your toes, on your heels, with your feet pointing towards one another, or jump with your feet together...

** Your child practices observation and imitation as well as balance and precise movements.

18

Miss Mary Mack

Have two children stand face-to-face and link their hands — crossed over so that right hands are together and left hands are together. Now the children should begin marching — one forwards and the other backwards — while you sing:

Miss Mary Mack, Mack,
All dressed in black, black,
With silver buttons, buttons,
All down her back, back.

When you say "All down her back, back!" the children should turn their backs towards each other and march in rhythm in the opposite direction. The game can be repeated a few times. After some time, the children may learn the rhyme and may be able to recite it on their own.

**   This game helps children learn to take into account and adapt to the movements of a partner. It also helps to develop a sense of rhythm.

19

Basketball

Prepare a few balls of paper with your child, using, for example, old newspaper. Place a basket or box on a chair or small table, and then begin the fun, throwing the balls into the container! First try throwing from a short distance, and then little by little step back. Throw the balls with alternating hands or with both hands.

** Your child practices precise movements and throwing accuracy.

20
Cherry People

Cherries not only make good pretend-earrings, but also...people: with the head made from the pit, and the trunk, arms and legs from the stems. Glue everything onto a small piece of cardboard, and draw eyes, a nose and a mouth onto the pits. To make the people come alive, ask your child to move the cardboard gently.

---

* An inspiring game that shows a child how to create something interesting with very simple objects.

21

Foot Massage

This is a great game for the beach. Pour a little bit of water into a plastic bottle, and add a small amount of sand, then screw on the cap. Sit next to your child, and show her how to roll the bottle with bare feet, making everything inside mix. Take a break, and wait for the sand to settle, and then begin the game again.

** Despite what you may think, this game is rather difficult — your child needs to control the movements of her feet to keep the bottle from rolling away. It is an excellent exercise to prevent flat footedness.

22

The Lazy Cat

Your child pretends to be a cat while you recite the rhyme below. The recitation can be combined with gestures: your child pretending to sleep while you shake your finger.

Pussy cat, where have you been today?
In the meadows, asleep in the hay,
Pussy, you are a lazy cat,
If you have done no more than that!

** Thanks to this game your child develops his natural acting skills and exercises the memory.

23

Parrot

Place one of your child's toys in a characteristic pose, for example, a sitting doll with its arm raised as high as possible. Now ask your child to imitate the pose. When your child understands the game, change the doll's pose, and ask your little one to follow suit.

---

* This game teaches close observation, coordination and control of one's body.

24

Paper Necklace

For this activity, you will need a piece of drawing paper, glue, a crayon and colored crepe paper. Draw a circle on the paper, and ask your child to rip off pieces of the crepe paper and roll them into little balls — 'diamonds'. Now they can be glued onto the circle you have drawn. Let your child complete this task in any way she wishes to gain a real feeling of individual accomplishment that mom or dad can be truly proud of.

** Develops manual dexterity and creativity.

25

Buried Treasure

When you are with your child in a sandbox or on the beach, you can play at looking for buried treasure. Ask a few other children to join in the search. Agree on what treasure you want to find: maybe a sand mould or a shell. Have one child hide the treasure in a mountain of sand and create as many piles of sand as there are children searching for it, while the other children turn away. Now each child can choose one pile of sand and start searching for the treasure. The child who finds it wins and hides it in the next round.

---

* A team game that teaches children simple rules of behavior while playing with others.

26

We All Fall Down

Have a group of children stand in a circle and hold hands, turning while they recite the well-known rhyme below:

Ring-around the rosie,
A pocket full of posies.
A-tishoo! A-tishoo!
We all fall down!

At the words "Fall down!" the children fall over while trying to hold onto each other's hands to maintain the circle. This is a game that can be played over and over, creating lots of laughs and happiness!

** A game that develops a sense of rhythm, exercises the memory, teaches cooperation with others and builds emotional connection.

27

Flying Feather

Throw a feather into the air, and blow on it from below. When it begins to fall, ask your child to join the game by blowing on the feather to keep it in the air as long as possible. Encourage your child to experiment by blowing hard or gently, from the side or from below.

---

* A simple game that allows your child to exercise breathing.

28

Dress Up

Although a two-year-old may not be able to dress without assistance, your child will certainly enjoy trying on different articles of clothing. The real fun begins when your child decides to put gloves on feet, or socks on hands, or even wear one of your hats. Throw in a child's shirt, skirt or shorts, and let your little one's imagination run wild!

*** Develops the ability to dress and undress oneself, awakens the imagination and creates lots of laughs.

29

Larger than Life

Explain to your child how to look through a magnifying glass, and make sure he can manipulate this tool. If so, provide a variety of objects for your child to examine, e.g., a drawing, a piece of fruit, your hand... Then go outside, and let your little one look at the grass, flowers, leaves, insects — the world of nature magnified will be an incredible discovery!

---

* A game that satisfies your child's thirst for exploration and allows him to see the world differently.

30

Blanket Fun!

This game is for a group of children. Throw a blanket high in the air, asking the children to run to wherever it lands. The winning child is the one who is able to get under the blanket first.

---

* During this game, children develop observation skills and reflexes as well as get a taste of competition.

31

Finger Painting

A two-year-old is just beginning to learn how to hold a crayon and use it to draw, but will have no problem creating a 'picture' with fingers dipped in paint. Prepare a sheet of paper, paint and water. Put newspapers down to protect the table, then lay out the sheet of paper, and invite your child to begin. Don't forget to dress your little artist in a protective smock.

---

*   Exercise that develops the imagination using little fingers.

32

Rhyming

Children love rhymes and love to recite them. Teach your child the rhymes below, and demonstrate how to clap in rhythm.

Baa, baa, black sheep,
Have you any wool?
Yes, sir! Yes, sir! Three bags full!
One for the master,
One for the dame,
And one for the little boy who lives down the lane.

Diddle, diddle, dumpling, my son John,
Went to bed with his trousers on;
One shoe off, and one shoe on,
Diddle, diddle, dumpling, my son John!

* Develops memory and a sense of rhythm.

33

Gardener

Ask your child to play gardener. Prepare a small container of water, and allow your child to choose an onion. Help your little one put the onion in the container so that it sticks up out of the water. Explain how chives grow from the onion, and emphasize that this process takes time. It is also a good occasion to mention why chives are healthy to eat and what they taste best with.

---

*   An early lesson about nature and patience.

34

Beach Truck

Pour some sand into a bucket, and set it gently on your child's back. The challenge is to crawl on all fours in order to transport this 'load' to a specific place, e.g., daddy's beach chair.

*** Your child learns to maintain balance and coordinate movement.

35

Sky in Movement

This game requires two adults and any number of children. The adults hold each side of a large piece of material: a blanket, beach towel, sheet or scarf. Turn on some music. When the music is playing, the children should dance, but once it stops they should hide under the 'sky' as fast as possible. A special music mix can be prepared ahead of time, e.g., music of various speeds, volumes and genres, etc.

** A physical game that develops physical fitness and hones reflexes.

36

Itsy, Bitsy Spider

Present this funny rhyme, changing your voice and facial expression — you are an actor and your child is the audience. Then encourage your child to perform in front of an assembly of dolls and stuffed animals: repeating the text after you, using the accompanying gestures. When the presentation finishes, praise your child and share some hugs.

The itsy, bitsy spider went up the water spout;
Down came the rain and washed the spider out.
Out came the sun and dried up all the rain,
And the itsy, bitsy spider went up the spout again!

THE ITSY, BITSY SPIDER!

---

* A game that develops a sense of humor and familiarizes your child with abstract situations.

37

Open Wide, Guess what's Inside!

Put one of your child's toys into a sack or box without revealing which toy it is. Start the game with these words: "Open wide, guess what's inside!" Your child should reach into the sack or box (without looking), and using touch, try to guess which toy is hidden inside. Then switch roles. Ask your child to put another toy into the sack and let you guess what is inside.

** A game that hones the sense of touch and teaches patience.

38
Fall Leaves

While walking children often collect leaves — try to use them for a fun activity. Prepare the best specimens, and dry them carefully in a pile of books. When they are dry, prepare sheets of drawing or construction paper, paintbrushes and paint. Ask your child to paint the leaves using the color she chooses, and then press the leaves onto the white paper to create a beautiful composition.

✶✶ Your child creates an original piece of art independently by choosing colors and shapes. This activity awakens the imagination and sensitizes a child to the beauty of nature.

39

Bridge

Lie down on the floor with hips raised as high as possible, and support yourself with your arms and legs. Ask your child to crawl under the 'bridge' from one side to the other. This game can last as long as the bridge can stand!

---

*   A game that develops a child's fine motor skills and awakens the imagination.

40
Freight Cars

You will need a set of your child's blocks — all with the same shape and only in two colors, e.g., green and red. Tell your little one that the blocks represent freight cars and put them into the following order: green – red – green – red. Once your child understands the pattern, encourage him to help you by finishing the 'train'. Eventually, you might want to add more colors to increase the level of difficulty.

**   This game helps your child learn colors, develop observation skills and hone concentration.

41

Head, Shoulders, Knees and Toes!

Head, shoulders, knees and toes;
Knees and toes.
And eyes and ears and mouth and nose;
Head, shoulders, knees and toes;
Knees and toes.

Sing or say this rhyme, touching the appropriate parts of your body, and invite your child to follow your lead. Your child might not be able to follow everything at first, but after a few repetitions will learn it well. This activity will be even more fun with a larger group of children. You can also experiment with the liveliness of the rhyme by speeding it up or slowing it down.

** A game that develops careful listening and reflexes.

42

Almost like the Circus!

Tell your child about the circus, and propose a game of tightrope. Lay out a long piece of rope or string on the floor, and demonstrate how to walk over it, putting one foot in front of another. Ask your child to do the same — it will be easier to balance with arms extended. Walking backwards over the string is a bit more difficult, but do encourage your little one to try. Once your child has mastered these tasks, create bends in the string for a bigger challenge. Your child can pretend to be a car on a racing track.

** Develops balance.

43

Lula! Bula!

This is a game for two. Count loudly to three, and then you and your child, each shouts one of two words: "Lula!" or "Bula!" If you shout a different word (e.g., you shout: "Bula!" and your child: "Lula!"), repeat the game again until you both shout the same word. If you manage to shout the same word twice, reward yourselves with a tasty treat.

---

* Lots of fun and joy!

44

Mr. Bear

For this game, you will need a musical instrument — either a toy that makes music or a household item that makes a distinctive noise — which represents the bear's honeypot. One child is chosen to be the 'bear', and the rest sit in a circle around him. Then the children sitting in the circle sing this rhyme:

Isn't it funny how bears like honey?
Buzz, buzz, buzz.
I wonder why he does.
Go to sleep, Mr. Bear.
Don't peep, Mr. Bear.

At this the bear pretends to sleep. Meanwhile, one child sneaks into the circle and takes the 'honeypot', sounds it and hides it behind his back. Then everyone shouts: "Wake up, Mr. Bear, someone has stolen your honey!" The bear has to guess who is hiding the honeypot, based on where the sound came from, and if he guesses correctly, the child who took the honeypot becomes the bear in the next round.

---

* An excellent game for developing listening skills!

45

My Puzzle

Prepare a puzzle by printing out a large picture of your child and gluing it onto a sheet of cardboard. Then cut this into several pieces to create a simple puzzle. Ask your child to reconstruct the portrait. Once the task becomes too easy, cut these larger pieces into smaller fragments.

✳✳ Develops memory, observation skills and spatial imagination.

46

Splash!

Pour water into a bucket, and place it in front of your child a short distance away. Give him a plastic ball, and instruct your child to throw it into the bucket. Every time the ball lands in the water, congratulate your child with the words: "Splash! Splash!" Your child will certainly delight in repeating these words. This game is best played outside: remember to dress in clothing that can get wet.

** A game that develops coordination and is a lot of fun.

47

Modeling Clay

Draw a large simple picture on a piece of paper — ideally with a large marker so that the lines are very visible. Give your child some modeling clay to first form little balls, and then using his fingers, to flatten and spread the clay onto the paper, inside the shape you have drawn. This work of art will be both impressive and original!

** A fantastic exercise for fingers that also develops a child's creativity.

48

Crazy Faces

This is a game for you and your child, but it can also include other participants. Stand in front of a mirror, and make various faces: scary, funny, sad, angry, surprised, etc. For example, open your mouth wide, stick out your tongue and grin. The children will definitely surprise you with their ideas, and the game guarantees a lot of laughs!

---

* While releasing excess energy, children are given an opportunity to exercise the muscles of the face, relax and have fun. It also awakens creativity.

49

Hot and Cold

If you're planning to give your child a gift, make it a game. Hide the present somewhere, and then ask your child to find it. You can help by saying "Cold!" or "Ice cold!" when your child gets farther away, and "Warm!" or "Hot!" as she approaches it.

** A game of logical thinking that hones observation.

50
What Hurts?

Have your child select a toy like a doll or stuffed animal — this is the sick patient that needs to be treated. Name various parts of the body while your child touches them with a magic wand that you have already prepared (a small stick or straw) and...the patient is all better! Then change roles: have your child pretend to be sick and tell you what hurts, and let the doll (with your help) make it all better.

---

* Your child learns proper pronunciation, develops memory and learns the names of parts of the body.

51

Tunnel

Prepare a few large boxes, ideally of the same size. Cut out two sides of each box to create openings. Then place the boxes next to each other to create a tunnel. The point of the game is to go from one end of the tunnel to the other and will be even more fun with a larger group of children. The boxes can also be used as hiding places or boats, and your child can also become a ghost by putting one of the boxes on her head...

---

* A game that develops imagination and awakens creativity.

52

Wild Animals

This is a game that captures a child's attention. It is based on saying (or singing) the following rhyme while your child carries out the actions described, i.e. pretending to eat, climb or jump.

I can see a panda eat bamboo.
I can see a panda eat like you. (Action: eating)
I can see a monkey climb up a tree.
I can see a monkey climb like me. (Action: climbing)
I can see a kangaroo jump in the zoo. (Action: jumping)
Can you?

** This game helps a child learn pronunciation and the names of animals; it develops imitation skills and hones the imagination. It can also be repeated with other animals and actions.

53

Stomp

This is the best way to pass a rainy day: take some shoes out of the closet — as many as there are players. Have them lay out their own shoe, one after the other, but not necessarily in a straight line as you don't have to choose the shortest route. The one who wins is the first to get his or her shoe out of the room.

---

*   A great physical activity that teaches patience and how to win and lose.

54

Let's Play Ball

This is a game for adults and children to play together. Participants sit next to one another on the floor with legs extended to create an unfinished circle. One person rolls the ball towards the other, who rolls it to the next and the next, etc. The game continues as long as the ball remains in the circle.

---

*   Thanks to this game, your child trains dexterity and learns how to accurately roll a ball.

55

Scribbles

Tape a piece of paper to the wall, and give your child a crayon, marker or pen. Ask him to cover it with scribbles. These can include straight lines, dotted lines or wiggly lines — lightly or vigorously drawn. Then propose drawing with two hands. This is a real challenge at this age! If your child doesn't want to continue with both hands, he can put one crayon down and keep drawing.

** An exercise in concentration and coordination.

56

Breakfast Rhyme

Eggs, butter, bread.
Eggs, butter, bread.
I'm so very hungry,
And I'd love to be fed!

Your child often has more interesting things to do than eat a meal, so invite him to the table with this happy rhyme. With time this rhyme will be so familiar that your little one may say it alone before eating. The names of the foods can also be changed depending on whatever is being served.

---

*   A game that exercises memory and teaches discipline.

57

Marco Polo

This game is ideal for a large group of children and guarantees fun. Cover one child's eyes with a blindfold, and make sure he can't see anything. The other children can then spin this child around to confuse the sense of orientation. Then the other children run away while the blindfolded child looks for them. In order to find them, this child says "Marco!" to which the other children must reply "Polo!" The child who gets caught is then blindfolded in turn.

---

*   This game teaches children control over their bodies, trains reflexes and orientation.

58

Hide-and-Seek

Try this game together: first you seek. Stand against a wall, cover your eyes and slowly count to ten. When you finish, say: "Ready or not! Here I come!" During this time, your child should have looked for a place to hide. Find your child and then change roles.

---

*   This popular game is a test of your child's creativity and a source of unforgettable fun.

59

Shapes

Cut several different sizes of circles, triangles, squares and rectangles out of colored paper. Now try with your child to put them in order according to a certain pattern: select shapes of the same color, then the ones of the same size or shape. You can finish by gluing all of the shapes on a piece of cardboard — creating your child's unique composition of colors and shapes.

** Teaches your child about geometric forms and abstract thinking, aids memorization of colors and hones observation skills.

60
Charades

Charades is a classic pantomime game that should be simplified for kids who are just learning to play. Invite your child to release his natural acting ability in imitating different animals, activities such as sweeping the floor or characters such as a crying baby. This is also a great activity for a group of children.

** A game that aids in the development of speech, gives a child an outlet for expression and is also good physical exercise.

61

Pocket Treasure

Children love to collect chestnuts, acorns, sticks... Hide some of these treasures in your pockets, and ask your child to look for them — by touching or asking questions — but not to look into your pockets.

** A game that develops observation skills, teaches logical thinking and helps parents and children bond.

62

Who's First?

This is a game for at least three people. One person takes the lead in making a gesture, e.g., pinching his nose. The other players must follow suit by pinching their own noses as fast as possible. The one who reacts last becomes the leader and pinches another part of the body. This is a simple game that brings relaxation and fun.

---

* A very good exercise for improving physical condition, speed and coordination.

63

Pat-a-Cake

Pat-a-cake, pat-a-cake, baker's man,
Bake me a cake, as fast as you can;
Pat it, prick it, and mark it with B,
Put it in the oven for baby and me.

Have your child sit on your lap, and clap your hands together while saying this rhyme. After a while, your little one will learn the words by heart and will be able to recite it while clapping against your hands.

---

* A game that develops dexterity, balance, memory
and the bond between parent and child.

64

Quiet, Loud

This is another version of the classic game 'hot and cold'. Hide an object in a place that is accessible to your child, and ask him to search for it. You can help by saying the name of the object louder or more softly — depending on how close your child is to discovering it.

** This game practices good observation and stimulates intelligence and physical fitness.

BLUE

65

A World of Colors

Choose a color among those that your child knows, and ask him to bring you an object of that color. You can also indicate an object and ask your child to name its color.

** Thanks to this exercise, your child learns to recognize colors and develops observation skills.

66

Bad Kitty

Ask your child to behave like an unruly kitten chasing a mouse around the room. Your part of this game is to pretend to worry that the cat will knock over everything it comes across and try to catch it. Your child can run away on all fours or hide behind furniture, etc. Switch roles once the cat has been caught.

---

*　Trains your child's coordination.

67

Small, Bigger, Biggest

Putting things in order is an important skill in life and worth developing during the early years. This time ask your child to put a series of objects in order by size. If you are playing outside, you could use rocks or blocks, or pieces of fruit for indoor play.

** An activity that develops intelligence and logical thinking, teaches independence and decision-making.

68
Frogs

Draw a large circle (chalk on the sidewalk; stick on the sand; at home you can create a circle on the floor by laying out a string). The children should stand outside of the circle and prepare to jump. When you say "Frogs into the water!" they should jump into the circle. If you say "Frogs on shore!" no one should move. The winner is the player who isn't fooled by this second command.

---

*   Thanks to this game, children learn to listen carefully and react quickly.

69

An Unusual Album

When the weather does not permit a walk outside, take time to prepare a unique album for your child with his hand and footprints. Use special body paint and sheets of paper in various colors. Allow your child to choose a color for painting his hand; stay close — you might need to help. First press your child's hand onto a piece of paper. Repeat this process using feet and then different colors of paint. When these 'stamps' are dry, the pages can be dated, bound together or framed. It will be a great gift for...your child's eighteenth birthday!

*   Just have fun!

70

Throwing the Handkerchief

This is a game for a group of children. All of the players stand in a circle, except for one child who is chosen to stand in the middle. The child in the center begins by throwing the handkerchief to someone in the circle. Whoever receives it must instantly throw it to someone else, and so on, while the child in the center tries to catch the handkerchief in its passage from one player to another. If he catches it, as it touches somebody, that child is now in the center. If the handkerchief is caught in the air, the player whose hands it left last enters the circle.

** A game that trains reflexes and develops physical dexterity.

71

Red Light, Green Light

Standing a few yards away from your child, turn your back and say: "Green light!" This is a signal to your child to start moving towards you in any way he decides. When you say "Red light!" and turn back towards your child, he must freeze instantly. By saying silly things, you can try to make your child laugh. If you succeed, your little one should return to the starting line, and the game begins again. When your child approaches close enough to touch you, switch roles.

***   Develops spatial imagination and control over one's body as well as reflexes.

72
Airplane

Lie down comfortably on the floor, bend your legs, and sit your child on your stomach. Spread wide, your child's arms become the wings of an aircraft getting ready for take-off. Now let the fun begin: lift your hips, sway them, extend your knees gently, and steer with the 'wings'. Make sure your child is securely balanced. The aircraft can land once you or your child is tired of the game.

---

* A game that develops balance and awakens the imagination.

73

Oink, Oink! Meow, Meow!

A game as old as time, but still well-loved by children. This time change the game: instead of asking what sound a pig makes, ask, for example, what animal goes "Oink, oink!" and so on.

---

* Develops a child's cognitive abilities and speech.

74

Spinning Top

Small children like to watch a spinning top. Wind one up if you have one, and let your child watch it go. Then pretend to be a top and spin around, either standing up or while sitting on the floor. Now ask your child to try it. Spin together — to the left, to the right — or one at a time until you say "Stop!"

Watch out: Your child may find it difficult to maintain balance alone and may need your help.

** Requires concentration and teaches balance.

75

Mealtime Rhyme

One, two, three, four!

_____ at the kitchen door. (Say your child's name)

Five, six, seven, eight!

Eating _____ off his/her plate! (Name the food your child is eating)

Before a meal, ask your child to take a seat at the table and close his or her eyes. Say this rhyme as you place your child's meal on the table. Food tastes better when it's a surprise!

---

* This is a time to enjoy — eating doesn't have to be a chore.

76

I Spy...

The next time you need to tidy up around the house, get your child involved with this cleaning game. Sit with your child in the middle of the room, and begin by observing what needs to be cleaned, e.g., "I spy with my little eye...a pile of blocks and a baby doll." Now encourage your little one to identify something that needs to be tidied. Once both of you are ready, the point of the game is to clean those items as fast as possible and return to the place where you were sitting. Your child will be motivated to get there first! This can be repeated as many times as needed and can include your partner or other children. Make cleaning a family affair!

** A game that builds up the parent-child bond, hones reflexes and teaches responsibility.

77

Guess which Hand

Hide a small object in your hand, e.g., a block or a small ball; hold both hands out in front of you, asking your child to guess which hand the object is in. If your child guesses correctly, switch roles. If not, hide the object again in one hand or the other, and encourage your child to try again.

** A game that hones reflexes and develops observation.

78
What's Next?

There are many simple household tasks that your child knows well: preparing meals, sweeping the floor, watering flowers... Tell your little one that you've forgotten how to carry out one of these tasks, and ask her to help you step by step. Only carry out the orders your child gives you that are correct and properly said.

** A game that teaches logical thinking, aids in developing more precise speech and gives a child a sense of importance.

79

Follow the Leader

This is a great game for a group of children, but can also be fun for two. Children love to imitate their caregivers. Have your child follow your lead, and add motor skills as you go along. Try walking on one foot, crawling, standing up, jumping, touching your toes, clapping hands above your head, and anything else you can think of. Adding funny faces and music is sure to make this game a favorite for your tot.

---

* Develops motor skills and careful observation as well as imitation.

80
Holiday Decoration

Prepare whole cloves and an orange. Cut the skin of the fruit with a sharp knife to create a happy face with eyes, eyebrows, a nose and a mouth. Show your child how to insert the cloves into these cuts, but before you do, allow her to smell this herb, and explain what it is called. The orange will release a pleasant smell over the holidays if placed near a heat source.

** Your child gains a sense of importance and pride by helping to prepare for the holidays and practices precise movements.

81

These Are my Eyes...

Touch your eyes, saying: "These are my eyes. Where are your eyes?" Continue in a similar way by naming other body parts — those your child already knows as well as new ones — encouraging your little one to follow you by identifying them.

---

* A fantastic educational game that helps children learn about parts of the body as well as develop listening skills.

82

Finish the Rhyme

Hold your child on your lap during a calmer moment, and start to recite a rhyme that your child knows well. Stop before the end of the rhyme, and allow your child to finish it for you. If he gets stuck, help — sooner or later your child will get it right.

** Your child learns proper pronunciation and develops its memory.

83

Giants and Dwarves

Have your child become a giant first by standing on tippy toes and stretching arms up as high as possible: a giant among giants! After a few moments in this position, have your child becomes as small as possible by kneeling down and rolling into a ball. When she is ready to become a giant again, repeat the process.

---

*   During this game, your child stretches and practices balance.

84
Cat and Mouse

This is a game for a larger group of children. While one child plays the mouse and another the cat, the others stand in a circle holding hands. The mouse stands inside while the cat on the outside of the circle tries to break through the circle and catch the mouse. If the cat catches the mouse, he wins the game, which can then be repeated with a new cat and mouse.

---

* Develops motor skills, orientation and reflexes, and allows children to experience an emotional thrill.

85

Mirror, Mirror

Stand with your child in front of a large mirror so that you both see each other's reflections. Make a face, and ask your child to imitate you, watching her own reflection and changing it to match yours. Try to combine a few different elements — for example, stick out your tongue, close one eye and pull on one ear.

** Your child learns to observe and imitate, trains facial muscles and learns about the possibilities of the human body.

86

Guess Who!

Print out your child's picture on a standard size sheet of paper. Find 'decorations' in color magazines, cutting them out and pasting them on the picture to create a hat, a different hair style, clothing, etc. Have fun together in composing a funny portrait by gluing on the elements your child chooses. This is an interesting piece of art that your child can show to other family members or guests who should guess whose portrait it is.

** Shapes the imagination, artistic ability and a sense of humor. Gluing also develops precision and patience.

87

Happy Animals

Cut out pictures of animals, cars and fruit out of colored magazines. Your child's task is to choose one group of photos, e.g., only animals. Together, spread glue onto the backside of each animal, and then let your child press each photo onto a piece of paper or cardboard. Depending on your child's favorite things, you can also prepare other photos for gluing, e.g., bears, flowers, etc.

*** Your two-year-old practices observation and the ability to associate facts as well as develops manual dexterity.

88

With your Partner

Sung to 'Skip to my Lou', turn in a circle:

With your partner, shake their hand.
With your partner, shake their hand.
With your partner, shake their hand.
Shake their hand, my darling!

Hold hands with your child to create a circle. A stuffed animal or doll can also be incorporated as another player. Any number of other verses is possible: turn around, stamp your feet, stand and bend, shake your hands, nod your head, march in place, and the best way to finish is: give a hug!

** Develops memory, including listening memory as well as a sense of rhythm, and develops the ability to play in a group.

89

Fly Away, Balloon!

Children love to hit and catch balloons. Normally, they do it with their hands, but not only. It can also be fun to hit the balloon with the legs, head, stomach or shoulder. This is a simple and safe game. Sometimes the balloon may unexpectedly burst. Explain this to your child, and make sure you have extra balloons on hand.

---

* A joyful game that allows your child to develop good reflexes.

90

Hello! Grandma?

Ask your child to call grandma or grandpa or someone else in the family. Before you assist him in dialing the number, unplug the phone — this is a game of pretend. Tell your child, for example, that he should recount something that has happened lately and then invite the person on the other end of the line to visit. Give your child free rein, for it is always possible that he has something important to say over the phone.

---

* By playing with the telephone, your child has a chance to express his thoughts and practice formulating them.

91

Grrrrr! Grrrrr!

During this game, your child is transformed into a dangerous animal, e.g., a tiger. Show your child how to sit on his heels and roar, open the mouth and stick out the tongue, show his teeth and show his claws. Obviously, you should look scared and shake in fear during this display.

---

* A very good exercise for the muscles of the face.

92

Monsters Galore

Monsters galore, can you roar? (Roar)

Monsters galore, can you soar? (Flying motions)

Monsters galore, please shut the door. (Clap)

Monsters galore, fall on the floor. (Sit/fall down)

This game involves reciting the rhyme while your child carries out the accompanying gestures.

---

* A game that improves coordination and allows a child to express emotions.

93

Let's Go Home!

Take a few rolled up socks — these will be the 'mice'. Place a small basket or box a short distance away, creating something like a little cave with the opening facing your child. Explain that the box is the nest. Your child's task is to return the mice to their home by rolling the socks into it.

*** Your child practices precise movements and shapes the imagination as well as has fun.

94
Night-Time Fun

In the evening when it gets dark, take your child to her room, and keep the light off. Give your child a toy to identify by touch alone. You can play along, not just by guessing and naming 'toys', but using other objects.

** Thanks to this game, your child becomes more comfortable with the dark.

95

Pattern

Find a thick string or piece of rope, and place it on a table in a simple pattern, e.g., a circle. Ask your child to watch while you do this. When you have finished, give your child the string, and ask her to try to make the same pattern. Once this shape has been mastered, try to make a wave, a spiral or whatever else comes to mind.

** A manual task that also develops careful observation.

96
Bunny-Hop

Small children love to run and jump! Show your child how a rabbit moves, and he will certainly imitate you. Next place a small stuffed animal, and jump over it like a rabbit. Now it's your child's turn to do the bunny-hop on hands and feet over this obstacle. Help him if needed.

** A great game that helps your child to develop coordination.

97

Five Little Puppies

Hold your child's hand open, palm facing up, as you recite this rhyme:

Five little puppies were playing in the sun.

(Then fold down each finger one by one)

This one saw a rabbit and he began to run. (First finger)
This one saw a butterfly and he began to race. (Middle finger)
This one saw a cat and he began to chase. (Ring finger)
This one tried to catch his tail and he went round and round. (Pinkie finger)
This one was so quiet; he never made a sound! (Thumb)

---

* A finger game that builds dexterity.

98

Puppet Show

For this game, you will need doll-size clothes or clothes that your child has outgrown — overalls or a bodysuit, socks, gloves — and a hat as well as pieces of scrap material — buttons, thread, cotton and a red marker. Use the scraps and cotton to make the puppet's head, sewing buttons on to create eyes and a nose, and draw on a mouth with the marker. With your child, fill the clothes with cotton, and then sew the head and body together. This doll can also be mounted to create a stick puppet that is perfect for theater games.

*   Your child enjoys the enormous satisfaction of having created his or her own doll.

99

Flying Lesson

Spread your arms wide, and ask your child to follow your lead as you pretend to be an airplane. Start to run, turning to the left or to the right, adding more difficult maneuvers as you go and announce them aloud. For example, as you slowly squat down, say: "The airplane is landing." Then slowly straighten your legs and say: "The airplane climbs higher." You can also experiment with imitating the sounds that an airplane makes. If your child's clothing has a pocket, he can also carry a small toy as a passenger!

---

*   Develops the imagination and teaches control over one's own body.

100

Five Red Apples

Five (four, three, etc.) red apples high in a tree.
One looked down and winked at me. (Wink at your child)
I shook that tree as hard as I could;
One fell down... Mmm, it was good!

Put on a kitchen apron with five red apples hidden in the pocket. Begin reciting the rhyme; as you drop an apple out gently for your child to catch, say: "One fell down." Repeat the rhyme, counting down the apples as the apron empties. Your child might know the rhyme by heart by the time the last apple falls.

** An excellent exercise of both memory and physical coordination.

101

The Hokey-Pokey

This game can be played in a larger group of children, or just you and your child. Either way, participants stand in a circle and carry out the motions to the corresponding words of the song. Two-year-olds might not know right from left at this point, but they will understand the body part and can follow your lead.

You put your left foot in.
You put your left foot out.
You put your left foot in, and you shake it all about!
You do the Hokey-Pokey, (Raise hands in the air and wiggle fingers)
And you turn yourself around. (Turn around in a full circle)
That's what it's all about! (Clap with each syllable)

Repeat the song with other body parts: arms, head, elbows, front side, back side, whole self.

** Helps children learn the names of body parts and how to follow directions.

Contents

Printed in Great Britain
by Amazon.co.uk, Ltd.,
Marston Gate.